The Window Cleaner

A play

Gillian Plowman

Samuel French—London
www.samuelfrench-london.co.uk

Copyright © 2007 by Gillian Plowman
All Rights Reserved

THE WINDOW CLEANER is fully protected under the copyright laws of the British Commonwealth, including Canada, the United States of America, and all other countries of the Copyright Union. All rights, including professional and amateur stage productions, recitation, lecturing, public reading, motion picture, radio broadcasting, television and the rights of translation into foreign languages are strictly reserved.

ISBN 978-0-573-02380-4

www.samuelfrench.co.uk

www.samuelfrench.com

For Amateur Production Enquiries

United Kingdom and World excluding North America

plays@samuelfrench.co.uk

020 7255 4302/01

Each title is subject to availability from Samuel French, depending upon country of performance.

CAUTION: Professional and amateur producers are hereby warned that *THE WINDOW CLEANER* is subject to a licensing fee. Publication of this play does not imply availability for performance. Both amateurs and professionals considering a production are strongly advised to apply to the appropriate agent before starting rehearsals, advertising, or booking a theatre. A licensing fee must be paid whether the title is presented for charity or gain and whether or not admission is charged.

The Professional Rights in this play are controlled by Samuel French Ltd, 24-32 Stephenson Way, London NW1 2HD.

No one shall make any changes in this title for the purpose of production. No part of this book may be reproduced, stored in a retrieval system, or transmitted in any form, by any means, now known or yet to be invented, including mechanical, electronic, photocopying, recording, videotaping, or otherwise, without the prior written permission of the publisher. No one shall upload this title, or part of this title, to any social media websites.

The right of Gillian Plowman to be identified as author of this work has been asserted in accordance with Section 77 of the Copyright, Designs and Patents Act 1988.

THE WINDOW CLEANER

Originally performed for Sphinx Theatre Company at Chelsea Theatre in November 2003 with the following cast:

Daryl   Daniel Harcourt
Jill   Jenny Maddox

Directed by Clare Lizzimore
Designed by Julie Landau

COPYRIGHT INFORMATION
(See also page ii)

This play is fully protected under the Copyright Laws of the British Commonwealth of Nations, the United States of America and all countries of the Berne and Universal Copyright Conventions.

All rights, including Stage, Motion Picture, Radio, Television, Public Reading, and Translation into Foreign Languages, are strictly reserved.

No part of this publication may lawfully be reproduced in ANY form or by any means — photocopying, typescript, recording (including video-recording), manuscript, electronic, mechanical, or otherwise — or be transmitted or stored in a retrieval system, without prior permission.

Licences are issued subject to the understanding that it shall be made clear in all advertising matter that the audience will witness an amateur performance; that the names of the authors of the plays shall be included on all announcements and on all programmes; and that the integrity of the authors' work will be preserved.

The Royalty Fee is subject to contract and subject to variation at the sole discretion of Samuel French Ltd.

In Theatres or Halls seating Four Hundred or more the fee will be subject to negotiation.

In Territories Overseas the fee quoted in this Acting Edition may not apply. A fee will be quoted on application to our local authorized agent, or if there is no such agent, on application to Samuel French Ltd, London.

VIDEO-RECORDING OF AMATEUR PRODUCTIONS

Please note that the copyright laws governing video-recording are extremely complex and that it should not be assumed that any play may be video-recorded for *whatever purpose* without first obtaining the permission of the appropriate agents. The fact that a play is published by Samuel French Ltd does not indicate that video rights are available or that Samuel French Ltd controls such rights.

CHARACTERS

Daryl, the burglar
Jill, the window-cleaner

The action of the play takes place in the sitting-room of an expensive flat.

Time—the present

AUTHOR'S NOTE

The play contains a few instances of explicit language. However, I have no objection if groups performing the play wish to substitute less strong language.

Gillian Plowman

*Also by Gillian Plowman
published by Samuel French Ltd*

The Allotment
Beata Beatrix
Cecily
Close to Croydon
David's Birthday
The Janna Years
A Kind of Vesuvius
Me and My Friend
Philip and Rowena
There's None So Blind
Tippers
Touching Tomorrow
Two Fat Men
Two Summers
Umjana Land

THE WINDOW CLEANER

The sitting-room of an expensive flat

There are some good pieces of furniture including a sofa, a chest of drawers and a telephone. Doors lead to the bedroom, the bathroom, the main entrance and the kitchen. There are windows

When the play begins, Daryl is looking through various drawers. He steals things from the drawers and puts the items into one of a few empty sports bags. He is dressed in tracksuit and trainers and could well be going to the gym

Jill, a window-cleaner, appears at the top of a ladder. She looks in while cleaning the outside of one of the windows. She has been given the keys by the estate agent to clean the windows whilst the owners are away. She is unattractive, with scraped-back hair, raw hands and raw face

They do not see each other

Jill finishes cleaning and disappears down her ladder. Daryl moves to the centre of the room with a full sports bag, zips it up and places it on the sofa. He picks up a second empty sports bag. He exits into the bedroom

Jill enters carrying an empty bucket with the word "Jack" painted on it. We see for the first time that she is wearing waterproof trousers over her jeans, and they creak as she walks. Her nose runs. She sniffs and tissues a lot. She inspects the windows, and goes out again, to get some water

Daryl returns

Daryl (*with shock*) Oohhh ...

Daryl is going to be sick and exits to the bathroom

The sounds of Daryl being sick and the loo being flushed are heard off stage

Jill creeps back in, still holding her empty bucket. She has heard the loo being flushed

Daryl bursts back into the room and slams the door shut. He turns to confront Jill

Daryl Aagh!
Jill Aagh ...
Daryl What!
Jill God!
Daryl Yes
Jill I thought it was empty
Daryl I've been sick. (*He wipes his mouth*)
Jill Where? (*She looks round*)
Daryl In the toilet. (*He gestures towards the bathroom door*)
Jill Has it got a window?
Daryl A window?
Jill The toilet?
Daryl I dunno.
Jill I'm the window-cleaner.
Daryl Are you?
Jill Agent gave me the keys. They said it was empty.
Daryl (*indicating*) Full of stuff.
Jill Full of stuff not empty, but like there's nobody here empty. Only there is.
Daryl Who?
Jill You.
Daryl Right. (*He looks towards the bedroom*)

Jill They're away, they said. South Africa, they said. Gone to look for somewhere there. For the winter. Well, their summer. Our winter. They'll come back here for our summer. Their winter. They get two summers and no winters ...
Daryl Does that seem right to you?
Jill If they can afford it.
Daryl One rule for the rich and another for the rest of us.
Jill If they've worked for it.
Daryl Some people don't need jobs at all. They get given money.
Jill Like asylum seekers?
Daryl No like rich gits!
Jill You gotta job?

Beat

Daryl Plumber. (*He grabs the bucket and sits with his head hanging over it*)
Jill What's the matter with you?
Daryl I've had a shock.
Jill You found a leak?
Daryl Yes.
Jill Turned off the stop cock?
Daryl What?
Jill Where's your tools?

Jill unzips his full bag before Daryl can stop her and looks inside

(*Realizing*) The agent said there's an inventory of all this stuff and they'll know if anything goes missing. You're daft ...
Daryl You turning up now was a very bad move.
Jill Looks like a very good move to me, as you haven't got a bucket.
Daryl You should not be here.
Jill The agent knows I'm here.

Beat

I'm supposed to be here.

Daryl (*looking up from the bucket*) So am I.
Jill They're worried about burglars. *They're* not supposed to be here.
Daryl Where they supposed to be then?

Jill looks at Daryl

If not in other people's houses?
Jill So you're a burglar?
Daryl No, I'm a plumber.
Jill With no tools.

Daryl turns to grab the bucket again

I'll get you a glass of water, shall I?
Daryl No.
Jill Settle your insides.

Jill runs for the kitchen door

Daryl No! (*He runs for the door and gets there before Jill*)
Jill Don't you want any water?

Daryl shuts the door

Daryl I said no. (*He grabs her*)
Jill Get off!
Daryl Scream and I'll slap yer.

Jill has a mobile in her pocket and trys to press the emergency button

Give us! (*He threatens*)

Jill takes her hands out of her pockets

Give us!

The Window Cleaner

Jill takes the phone out of her pocket and Daryl grabs it. He puts it down out of reach. He makes her move away from the kitchen door. She looks at another door

Sit on the floor. There.

Pause, neither of them knows what to do

Jill I don't know why you have to be so bossy.
Daryl What?
Jill It's not as if it's your house.
Daryl How do you know it's not?
Jill You don't know how to treat guests.
Daryl You're the fuckin' window-cleaner!
Jill Most people are grateful to have the fuckin' window-cleaner. *Most* people offer me tea and biscuits. And a chair.
Daryl Shut up!

Silence

Jill All right, we're both suffering from shock, finding each other here.
Daryl I'm trying to think.
Jill Not used to it?
Daryl Shut up.

Silence

Jill What do you do then?
Daryl Do you in a minute.
Jill Specialize in … ?
Daryl If you don't shut your mouth …
Jill Paintings? Silver?
Daryl Shut up!
Jill Anything you can get your hands on?
Daryl No. I'm choosy
Jill How did you get in?

Daryl Shut up!
Jill Any broken windows, I'll get the blame. That's not fair.
Daryl I didn't break any windows.
Jill Come down the chimney?
Daryl I might have a key. You've got a key.
Jill Why would you have a key? Don't tell me you're the plumber.
Daryl I might be someone who's looking after the place for them.
Jill Nicking their stuff.
Daryl Or a member of the family.
Jill But you're not.
Daryl How do you know?
Jill 'Cos you're nicking their stuff.
Daryl I'm the black sheep of the family.
Jill They'd have changed the locks.
Daryl They've got this house and a house in South Africa, and I get chucked out of my bastard little room if I don't pay the rent by today!
Jill You can get help.
Daryl What help?
Jill Social services.
Daryl You're joking! I'm helping myself. They've got all this and I've got nothing.
Jill Stealing it won't make it yours.
Daryl Yes it will, stupid. Mine to sell so I can pay the rent.
Jill You'll never have peace of mind.
Daryl Who's got that, eh, who's got it? Them, with their two houses, worried about burglars twice over now, you going into empty houses, not knowing who you might meet. Him ...
Jill Who?
Daryl Him ...
Jill Who?

Daryl looks towards the bedroom. Jill makes a bolt for the door but he trips her up and she falls to the ground. He pins her down. She struggles but he is much stronger and she is crushed and winded

Daryl I told you.

Jill nods. Daryl keeps her pinned down

Jill Please get off. I can't breathe. Don't make it worse.
Daryl You're making it worse. (*He keeps her pinned down*)
Jill Please. My bones will break and you'll have a dead body on your hands.
Daryl Oh. (*He rubs his head as if it is hurting*)

Jill pushes herself away from him along the floor away from the door

  Just stay there

Jill watches him. Daryl shrugs, vaguely apologetic. He paces

Jill Special key is it?
Daryl What?
Jill They've put in a new security system, which turns off when you put the special key in the door.
Daryl It wasn't *on*.
Jill How did you get in?
Daryl Just fuck off, will you.
Jill Sure.

Jill starts to go and Daryl stops her

Daryl I don't mean fuck off, I mean fuck off. Sit down there and fuck off. You're a fuckin' pain. Stop yackin'!

Silence

  Door wasn't locked.
Jill Wasn't it? I'll get the blame for that, you know. Leaving the door unlocked. They'll say I was careless and negligent. I'll get the blame all right.
Daryl Not if you're dead.
Jill If I'm dead ... ?

Daryl Which you will be if you don't shut up.
Jill I only came to clean the windows ...
Daryl Do you wanna be dead?
Jill I'm not sure.
Daryl Not sure?
Jill Dead's all right. Some people like it.
Daryl How do you know?
Jill They have a smile on their face.
Daryl You won't have.

Beat

Jill I'd still get the blame if I was dead. That won't make any difference. They'll say I brought it on myself, leaving the door open. Letting people in. You can't trust anyone these days. Do you find that?
Daryl No.
Jill I mean for example, you nick this bloke's computer, and he's got a load of child pornography on it, where you going to get rid of that if it's on the hard disc, eh? You could get done for that.
Daryl No, I wouldn't. I've just nicked his computer.
Jill With child pornography on it.
Daryl That's disgusting.
Jill They'll pin it on you, don't you worry, and there you are in prison, not just for burglary but for possessing child pornography. So where are all your mates now? You won't last long inside or out. There's a case for liking to be dead.
Daryl Yeah
Jill I wouldn't take the computer.
Daryl I'm not.

Beat

Jill They'll be along soon to see if I've finished.
Daryl Don't try to be clever.
Jill What's clever about that?
Daryl Trying to trick me.

Jill See, that's what I mean.
Daryl What?
Jill No peace of mind. You're worried about me tricking you and you wouldn't be if you were doing a proper job.
Daryl You're the one who should be worried.
Jill I'm not 'cos they'll be along in a minute.

Daryl glares at Jill

Daryl Take them off.
Jill What?
Daryl Them. (*He points to her waterproof trousers*)
Jill Why?
Daryl They're noisy. Can't you hear 'em? Every time you move it does my head in.
Jill You've got a headache?
Daryl Yeah.
Jill Where?
Daryl In my head.
Jill Front? Back?
Daryl Down the sides. Both sides.
Jill Stress. (*She gets up*)
Daryl Take them off!
Jill Or what?
Daryl I'll slap yer.
Jill Do you treat everyone like that?
Daryl Just you trying to escape.
Jill I'm not trying to escape now, am I?
Daryl You might.
Jill I can run much faster without these on actually.
Daryl Shut up!
Jill Do you still want me to take them off?
Daryl Yes!

Jill does this clumsily

You'd never make a striptease artist.

Jill (*looking at the windows*) Filthy.
Daryl What?
Jill The windows. I've done the outside so all that's on the inside. You can hardly see out.
Daryl I can see out.
Jill You're looking *through* the windows. I'm looking at the windows. I don't suppose you've thought of windows in that way.
Daryl No. I look at them.
Jill Yeah?
Daryl To see what size brick you'd need to smash 'em.
Jill Plumbers don't smash windows.
Daryl No but firemen do.
Jill So you're a fireman now.
Daryl Could be.
Jill What's your name?

Silence

Gary? Simon? What difference does it make if you tell me?
Daryl Oh come on. Who else you going to tell?

Silence

Jill Let me get on.
Daryl Bloke's job.
Jill You reckon?
Daryl Window-cleaning.
Jill Why don't you do it then?
Daryl What?
Jill It's a mug's game, burgling. How many times you been caught? How many times you been in prison?
Daryl Dunno. Five times.
Jill See. What's the point?
Daryl That's what happens.
Jill *"That's what happens!"* Why does it happen? Haven't you got any control over your life? Haven't you got a brain? You don't

look disabled, but there must be something wrong in your head. *"That's what happens."* Don't let it happen. Do something about it.
Daryl I'm gonna do something about you! (*He starts towards her*)
Jill All right, all right. (*She zips her mouth shut*)

Beat

Look, why don't I just get on with the windows, and you get on with robbing? Call it quits.

Jill tries to go for the door once more but Daryl gets ahead of her. He loses his temper and thumps the door madly

Daryl No, no, no! Bloody stay where you are!

Jill grabs her bucket and tries to throw it at Daryl. He grabs it, puts it over her head and pins her arms to her sides. She screams inside the bucket. He has his arms round her, holding her immobile. He slowly lets go of her arms

Don't move. (*He takes a step in front of her*)
Jill I'm HIV positive!
Daryl What?
Jill HIV. I've got it. I've got AIDS.

Daryl takes the bucket off her head

Daryl What d'ya say that for?
Jill You ... 'Cos you ... I dunno.
Daryl You think I'm gonna ... ? You? The state of you? Not likely.
Jill You're not ... ?
Daryl No. You look better with it on!

Daryl puts the bucket back on her head and she sinks to the ground

Jill Why are you keeping me here then?

Daryl 'Cos you'll call the police.
Jill No, I won't.
Daryl (*derisory*) Huh!
Jill I've been in prison.
Daryl You have?
Jill Holloway.
Daryl What for?
Jill So I know what it's like.
Daryl What for?

Silence

Daryl bashes the bucket and Jill screams inside it

Silence

Daryl stares at the bucket, then turns it round to read it

Daryl Why does it say, "Jack"?
Jill Jack's the bucket?
Daryl Is it?
Jill My business name. Jack and Jill — went up the hill. It's hurting me — please.

Jill starts to take it off but Daryl holds it down with his hand

Daryl Who's Jill?
Jill Me.
Daryl You're Jill?
Jill Yes.

Silence

Daryl You all right?

Silence

You!

Silence

All right?

Daryl takes the bucket off. Jill is crying

Jill No, I'm not all right. You keep hurting me. (*She cries more*)
Daryl It's your own fault. Innit? Innit?
Jill No.
Daryl If you just did what I said.
Jill I don't want to. You're keeping me a prisoner and I don't want to do that.
Daryl But you've got to just — behave.
Jill I am behaving. Please don't hurt me any more.
Daryl You tried to get away.
Jill I've done nothing and you've hurt me.
Daryl I told you.
Jill You don't even know me.
Daryl So?
Jill I'm smaller than you.
Daryl Yeah?
Jill It's wrong. Hurting people smaller than you who have done no harm.
Daryl I don't want to ... ! I don't. I've got a little girl. I love her. I wouldn't want anyone to hurt her, ever. Even when I'm dead and she's old.
Jill If you can hurt me, someone can hurt your little girl. Just the same. And she's done nothing and I've done nothing and you'll make the world go round the wrong way.

Silence

What's *her* name?
Daryl Fred.
Jill Little girl?

Daryl Short for something.
Jill Fredericka?
Daryl Something like that.

Beat

Jill I haven't got anyone. Just Jack really. He's my — partner — my business partner.
Daryl He's a bucket.

Silence

Jill I know what it's like in prison and I don't understand why you want to keep going back.
Daryl The only reason I'll go back this time is if I let you blab.
Jill I won't blab.
Daryl So I have to stop you.
Jill I won't anyway.
Daryl Why not?
Jill I don't think it does anybody any good — prison. It's a habit. That's why you like it.
Daryl I don't!
Jill You do a job and you get caught and then you get punished. Go to prison. Serve your time. Clean slate. Start burglin' again. You've no control over your life. No conscience.
Daryl I never leave a mess.

Jill looks at Daryl

Jill What if you didn't get caught?
Daryl I don't always.
Jill And how does that feel?
Daryl Great. Straight great. Stupid bastards. They know who done it but they can't catch me. No proof.
Jill And then you do it again and you get caught.

Daryl shrugs

The Window Cleaner

They're not stupid. *You* are. They know you'll do it again. You want to fool them like I did.
Daryl You got caught.
Jill Only once. Then I didn't do it again. See, fooled them.
Daryl What did you do?
Jill I killed someone.
Daryl Killed someone?
Jill Yes.
Daryl Really?
Jill Yes.
Daryl Dead?
Jill Yes.
Daryl Who?

Beat

Jill Prison makes you worse. You come out worse than you went in. You can't keep doing that. You've got to change. I did.
Daryl There's a difference, isn't there? You can carry on doing poncy places like this, I mean — they'll just do the insurance company. You can't keep carrying on killing people. You done life then?
Jill Four years.
Daryl How d'you get away with that?
Jill Mitigating circumstances.
Daryl I don't believe any of it. You're an ugly little cow and you're winding me up.
Jill Why would I?
Daryl 'Cos you want to get on the right side of me.
Jill I want to get out of here.
Daryl Exactly.
Jill We could both just get out of here.
Daryl No 'cos ...
Jill What?
Daryl 'Cos.
Jill Am I ugly?
Daryl Yes.

Jill Right.

Beat

Daryl Look at the state of your hands.
Jill My hands?
Daryl How did they get like that?
Jill Window-cleaning.
Daryl You never heard of rubber gloves?

Jill looks at her hands

Jill What does it matter to you?
Daryl My wife had beautiful hands. White, soft with fingernails — she used to paint pictures on her fingernails, they were so long.
Jill Your wife dead then?
Daryl What?
Jill *Had* beautiful hands. Or have they fallen off?
Daryl What?
Jill Like Greek statues. Their hands fall off.
Daryl No her hands didn't fall off and she's not dead.

Beat

> She didn't like flaunt anything — I would watch her. With men, you know. She'd laugh and put her hand on their arm and they would look at those nails and, and feel them digging into their sleeve and — I never hurt my wife. She was beautiful. I didn't want to spoil her. She left me. (*He looks at her hands*) Imagine *them* on your arm.

Jill puts one hand on her other arm for a moment

> Disgusting!

Pause. Jill puts her hands behind her back

The Window Cleaner

Daryl *Are* you HIV positive?
Jill I could have been.
Daryl What?
Jill There was one bloke, you know, who thought I was all right. You know, he thought I looked all right and we got married. I had a white dress and ... (*she looks at her hands*) gold fingernails and twenty-seven people came. That's quite a lot isn't it? We knew quite a lot of people between us. So we set up this business — window-cleaning. He did the outside and called himself the Windows Maintenance Engineer. And I did the insides and was the Assistant Windows Maintenance Engineer.
Daryl Said it was a bloke's job.
Jill Something went wrong with him and he started hitting me. He kept saying I wasn't doing it properly, that I couldn't do anything properly, that I let him down like when we went out. He said I'd turned ugly. Like it's OK to hit ugly women. That's what you think, isn't it?
Daryl No!

Jill looks at him

Jill I was just the same as when we married ... Everybody said I was ... When he thought I was beautiful. I gave him headaches, he said.
Daryl I can imagine
Jill He had terrible headaches. And there was a reason.
Daryl You.
Jill The doctor sent him for tests. He wasn't faithful to me because I was ugly. Went with all sorts — prostitutes. And he got positive. So I could have got it.
Daryl How do you know you haven't?
Jill Been four years in prison. They tested me several times. He didn't really want to do it with me but he wanted a son. To carry on the business.
Daryl And did he? You?
Jill No.
Daryl So where is he now?

Jill I don't know where people go. Do you?
Daryl What? When?
Jill When they've packed it in.
Daryl Packed what in?
Jill Window-cleaning.
Daryl What are you on about?
Jill He kept hitting me and — one day we were cleaning and he was up the ladder on the outside and I was doing the inside. And he was shouting at me — *ugly, ugly, ugly* — through the window, and there was such hate on his face. I opened the window and pushed the ladder. And he went backwards ... (*she moves her arm in a beautiful sweep*) in slow motion. Clinging to the ladder like he was performing in a circus. Hit his head. I can still see his face. The hate expression turned to amazement. He didn't believe it as he was going down. And he smiled just as he hit the ground. The smile stayed on his face.
Daryl It was him you killed?
Jill Tony Malpas. Convicted of the murder of Tony Malpas. And the thing was, he was dying anyway.
Daryl From HIV?
Jill No. From a brain tumour. That's why he was hitting me. 'Cos his personality was changed. It wasn't his fault ... See. Things aren't always what they seem.
Daryl What things?
Jill You'd think he was having a horrible death but there he was with a smile on his face so death must have been better ...
Daryl Better than what?
Jill Than living with HIV and a tumour, and me.
Daryl And your hands.
Jill You've got a thing about hands.
Daryl They do it, don't they?
Jill What?
Daryl They do the touching. When you think — don't they? Caressing. Like when two people are together.
Jill Don't.
Daryl No, no, I'm not ... Just looking at it, when you just look at it, it's her hands on you and your hands on her. You can't do it

The Window Cleaner

without hands like ... Hands like my wife. She taught me to keep mine smooth. Use cream. "You want to touch me ..."
Jill Don't.
Daryl Look. (*He shows her his hands*)
Jill Don't touch me!
Daryl I'm just showing you.

Jill hides her hands behind her back or under her armpits or under her clothes

Exactly. Exactly.
Jill Exactly what!
Daryl They're untouchables.
Jill Shut up!
Daryl And when you're bathing Fred, she said, you need smooth hands for Fred. (*He pulls her hands out*) If you had a baby, they'd bloody take it away from you with those hands.

Jill leaps at Daryl and he stumbles and falls. She crushes him with all her might, shaking him

Get off! You're hurting me.
Jill What do you know about it? What do you know about anything?
Daryl Aagh.
Jill See what it's like.
Daryl Calm down.

Jill gets the bucket and rams it on his head

Jill I had a baby.
Daryl Oh!
Jill And they took it away from me!
Daryl Told you.
Jill It wasn't because of my hands! It was because I'd killed the father and she was born in prison.

Daryl takes the bucket off his head

Daryl But you're out. Haven't you got her back. Haven't you?
Jill No.
Daryl No, because ... (*He nods at her hands*) No, I'm sorry ... Why haven't you got her back?
Jill How's your headache?
Daryl Killing me.
Jill Could be.
Daryl Does it look like the headaches he had?
Jill Pretty much.
Daryl How long did he have them?
Jill About a year.
Daryl Till he died?
Jill Yes.
Daryl I've had mine about a year.
Jill Ah well.
Daryl Ah well what?
Jill You work it out.
Daryl Do you think I've got a tumour?
Jill Well there's something wrong with your head, isn't there, that you can't see how stupid you're being. Keeping me here is making your head worse.
Daryl You rammed a bloody bucket on it.
Jill Hurting me is going against your nature, you say. Your body's all tensed up. You'll get constipation next.
Daryl Oh bloody hell!
Jill Let me clean the windows and you put everything back so's nobody can tell you've been here and we both just go.
Daryl I don't trust you.
Jill Everybody else does! I had five houses to do today. I won't get many done at this rate. I'll lose that trust. And I'll lose business. *Why can't you see?*

Pause

Daryl So how much do you get? Five houses?
Jill I get fifty quid a house.
Daryl Really?

The Window Cleaner

Jill If I do inside as well.
Daryl In a day?
Jill Yes.
Daryl So how much do you get in a day?
Jill Five times fifty quid.
Daryl Yeah?

Pause

Jill Two hundred and fifty.
Daryl In a day?
Jill How much do *you* get?
Daryl Depends. Every day?
Jill If I want.
Daryl Seven days a week?
Jill Yes.
Daryl That's — that's ...

Pause

Jill One thousand seven hundred and fifty quid a week.
Daryl What do you do with it?
Jill What do *you* get?
Daryl Bloody window-cleaning, eh ... ?
Jill Can't go to prison for window-cleaning.
Daryl A week!
Jill Providing you don't get stuck in a house with someone who won't let you out.
Daryl I'd sort them.
Jill You *are* them.
Daryl Yeah.
Jill So how am I going to sort you?
Daryl I don't mean me.
Jill You won't let me go and do my five houses.
Daryl No, because — because!
Jill What?!
Daryl Because I haven't decided.

Jill See, you have to promise to do what you say you'll do or you won't get any more houses

Beat

Daryl All right. You can do in here.

Jill points to the bedroom door

Jill What's through there?
Daryl Bedroom.
Jill How many windows? (*She goes to look*)
Daryl No! (*He stops her*) Do in 'ere.
Jill I need some water.
Daryl We'll get it together.

They go out the main door

Her mobile phone rings

Jill comes running back in followed by Daryl who is carrying rubber gloves. She grabs the phone

Don't answer it! (*He snatches it off her and throws her the gloves*) Put them on.
Jill They're ringing to check.
Daryl Put them on or I'll slap yer. (*Pause*) Just put 'em on.

Jill puts the gloves on

(*Listening to the phone message*) They hoped the key worked. Ring if there are any problems. (*He puts the phone into his pocket*)
Jill That's bloody useful, isn't it? Ring if there are any problems. The problem is I can't ring to tell them there are problems and that's the problem! (*She starts to clean the windows*)

Daryl opens more drawers

I assume Fred doesn't live with you.

Daryl No. With her mum.
Jill Do you see her?
Daryl I don't know whether to or not.
Jill You don't see her?
Daryl Sometimes.
Jill She's your daughter.
Daryl That's the problem, innit.
Jill What?
Daryl Her mum fancied someone else so she's got a new dad. Her mum says not to confuse her. Better off not seeing her so she doesn't get confused. I'm allowed to. One day a month I'm allowed at the moment. Her mum says if I go inside again, she'll go to court to get that day stopped. I might as well not bother at all. To see her. Best ...
Jill For Christ's sake, of course it's not best! You can't be bothered?
Daryl I didn't mean I can't be bothered.
Jill I might as well not bother, you said.
Daryl I want to give her things. I want to give her everything she wants.
Jill It's not things she wants — it's you. You being bothered. You being there for her.
Daryl I'm not allowed to.
Jill How pathetic is that? The minute you say you might as well not bother, you've given up on her. You're evading your responsibilities. You're going for the easy option, the "that's what happens they won't let me" option.
Daryl I'm trying to keep my bedsit, so I *can* see her.
Jill By robbing? Risking going inside again? You're not the victim here, you know, Fred is.
Daryl That's what I said to her mum. If you take her away from me, she'll miss me.
Jill What did she say?
Daryl She'll get over it.

Pause

Jill Did you love her mum? Or just her fingernails?

Daryl I don't know. I did. Yeah I did. But she was too beautiful to keep. I always knew that so I tried not to love her. Then after she was gone, I loved her so much. It ... I dunno.
Jill Hurt.
Daryl Yeah. Like a stomach ache. Did you love him?
Jill I did. Then I didn't. Then after I killed him, I did again and — like you ...
Daryl It hurt.
Jill Like a stomach ache.
Daryl Fred, she takes after her mum.
Jill What, fingernails?
Daryl She's in here. (*His clenched fist rests on his gut*)
Jill Don't let her go. You shouldn't have let her mum go.
Daryl I couldn't stop her. She was ...
Jill What?
Daryl Bored.

Pause

Jill You should go to court and fight for more time with Fred. You could — if you weren't a stupid sodding burglar. If you were a fireman ...
Daryl Well, I'm not.
Jill You could be. What if your day with Fred is pouring with rain?
Daryl Usually is.
Jill All you've got to remember is a wet day. And then it's wet again the next month.

Daryl shakes his head

Daryl Best.
Jill No! She knows you're her dad! Just stop all this and even if you haven't got a job, go to court and say you're looking for one and that you want her for whole weekends so you can carry on being her dad. That you'll never smack her.
Daryl Never. Never. I would never do that. I'm not violent. Her mum smacks her. Her mum hit me, I tell you, I tell you.

The Window Cleaner

Jill When?
Daryl The last time there was a burglary and the police came round our house to question me. But no, it's not like what you think. Me — I can take care of meself but this, with you, is not like — me and her — even when ——
Jill What?
Daryl — she wanted somebody else. "Slap her," they said, my mates ...
Jill Don't listen.
Daryl You got to show her who's boss.
Jill You've got to be equal.
Daryl And we weren't.
Jill Because men are bigger and stronger and they hit women.
Daryl We weren't equal because I loved her more than she loved me.
Jill But she doesn't love Fred more than you do.
Daryl No.
Jill So you gotta tell them.
Daryl Do you know how long you have to wait?
Jill So wait. It's for more days with Fred.

Daryl opens a drawer to find it full of twenty pound notes

Daryl Bloody hell!
Jill What?
Daryl Jackpot!
Jill It's a trap.
Daryl What?
Jill For me. It's a trap. How much do you reckon is there?
Daryl Couple of thou'.
Jill See?
Daryl No.
Jill If you were a window-cleaner and you came in and had a nose round and found that, what would you do? And you wanted to keep your job and your reputation and five houses a day. What would you do?

Daryl thinks long and hard

Daryl Leave it there?
Jill Correct.

Daryl starts to pocket it

Daryl Yeah well I'm a burglar.
Jill You're going to give that up.
Daryl Give it up after this.
Jill You leave it there, and you let me go and you put everything back and they can't get you. Fooled 'em ...
Daryl And then you give them a description.
Jill No. I clean the windows and go and you and me, we're square. Why would I give them a description when you haven't done anything?
Daryl I could steal it and we could share it.
Jill Put it back.

Daryl is drooling over the money

Daryl I can't.
Jill Yes you can.
Daryl It's fallen into me lap. It's meant to be.
Jill No, it's not.
Daryl It would hurt me something chronic to put it back.
Jill Let it!

Daryl holds his hands to his head as if it is hurting

Daryl I've got to pay me rent.
Jill You've got to make decisions.
Daryl No, I haven't.
Jill We can't stay here forever.
Daryl It's better than my place. How long are they away for? (*He puts all the money in his bag*)
Jill What if it's a trap for you?

Daryl What?
Jill Your fingerprints are all over the notes. You keep going on about rubber gloves. Why aren't you wearing them?
Daryl They won't check these for fingerprints.
Jill Special notes. Put them in a till and they activate an alarm. They get checked and there they are, your fingerprints.
Daryl How did they know I would be here?
Jill All burglars. They're out to get all burglars. They'll stop at nothing. Now what are you going to do? Give them to Fred? See how she copes with being questioned by the law?
Daryl They wouldn't.
Jill They would.
Daryl I mean, how is it — my wife and I, we get a house and we have Fred, and I'm faithful to her — I don't look at another woman, then she fancies someone else and I have to leave the house and she gets to keep Fred, and on my day with Fred, she's often doing something else or gone somewhere and my wife doesn't say it's your day with your dad so you can't do something else, she lets her ... How is all that? And I can't do anything about it.
Jill You can!
Daryl And they write and tell her and she takes no notice. Fred's ill today, and — last time — she said Fred doesn't want to see you.
Jill Did she say that?
Daryl And I couldn't ask her myself because I went to meet her after school and my wife called the police and said I was harassing her and the police said it wasn't my day with Fred. And they can't *make* my wife let her see me, like it wouldn't be good for Fred if they sent her to prison for defying court orders. So they don't do anything.
Jill Do you know what I shouted?
Daryl What?
Jill As he went down. (*She repeats the beautiful sweep arm movement*)
Daryl The law doesn't care about fathers.
Jill I'm pregnant, I shouted. I'm pregnant. That's why he was smiling.

Daryl Nobody cares about fathers.

Jill Nobody cared about me either. You know those twenty-seven people that came to our wedding? They disappeared. The only one person who was at our wedding who came to see me in prison was my mum, and I begged her to have my baby, and my mum said, "No." My mum said, "No." My mum said, "No." You can't keep a baby in prison and my mum said, "No." "She'll be going to school by the time you get out of here," my mum said, "and she won't know you from..." "But she'll know you," I said, "and you can keep her for me", but it was all to do with the social workers and my mum's non-compliance.

Daryl I told you about social workers.

Jill It was my mum! They would have let her.

Daryl And your dad ... ?

Jill My mum never told me who he was, and that's why she was non-compliant because she just had me and look what happened to me, and that's what would happen to my little girl, and the best thing was for her was to be adopted by a normal husband and wife who wanted a baby and couldn't have one, and she would have the best of everything and not be like me. So what's the point of having hands when I haven't got my little girl! (*She takes the rubber gloves off*) They took her away. I don't know where she is now. She had blue eyes and I called her Bluebell, but they changed it because they knew that when I got out I would be looking for all the Bluebells in the country that could be my little girl. I work, that's all, work and save for her and — help people — because one day I know she'll want me to find her and she'll want to be proud of me. And you ... And you — you're just whining on about your wife not letting you see Fred, and you know where she is, and you can hold her and hug her, and fight for her and you're her dad and she knows that you're her dad so don't give up on her. Don't even think it's best not to see her. She can't get confused because you're her dad and you'll do anything for her, and that means going straight and giving up this racket and being someone she can look up to. Because she knows who you are!

Beat

Daryl You get on with your windows.
Jill I've finished these. I need to do the other room now.
Daryl Yeah.
Jill I'll give you the rent money. I've got surplus. No-one to spend it on.
Daryl You should spend it on a week at a beauty farm. Or two. Or a year.
Jill It's a genuine offer. What do you need?
Daryl No! I don't know. I ... You're a ... I don't know ... Who do you think you are, going on at me, offering me money? You're just ... Just trying to ...
Jill What?
Daryl I dunno. Dunno. Like, I've never been in this situation before. I dunno.
Jill I've told you what to do.
Daryl Well you don't have the right to do that.
Jill And you don't have the right to keep me here with no ——
Daryl No what?
Jill Alternative.

Beat

Daryl We've both left finger-prints everywhere.
Jill Nobody's going to check them, are they, if nothing's out of place.
Daryl Except ...
Jill Clean the windows, put everything back and go. Lock up.

Daryl looks at the door to the bedroom

  What?
Daryl In there ...
Jill I'll go and do them.
Daryl Only ——
Jill What?

Daryl When that bloke fell off the ladder.
Jill My husband.
Daryl He was definitely dead?
Jill I told you
Daryl So you've seen a dead body?
Jill Yes.
Daryl Well there's another one in there.

She exits into the bedroom

Daryl is distinctly nervous and flips through the wad of the money a couple of times. There is silence from the bedroom

(*Shouting*) It's nothing to do with me. (*He flips through the money again*) I don't know who he is. He was there when I got here. I just found him. (*He puts the money back where he found it, then back into his bag*) I was just going to put everything back and go and then you turned up. (*He returns the money to the drawer once more*) Did you see it? I didn't see it at first. On the floor the other side of the bed. You could miss it. It's his feet sticking up.

Jill (*off*) Yes, very big feet.
Daryl Is he still dead? He must have — I mean ... Yes .... unlocked the back door ... Why there was no alarm ...*He* must be one of the family, mustn't he? Gone off the idea of South Africa.

Jill enters

Jill Gone off the idea of living.
Daryl You don't expect ... I mean ... You come in to get on with a job and there's a bleeding body staring at you ... So now you gotta get out ... Don't take anything and they won't know you've been ... Only now there's a fuckin' window-cleaner, and you have to *do* something ... (*He handles the money again and puts it back the drawer*) I'm putting it back. Look really, I don't know who it is. He was here ...
Jill Suicide.

The Window Cleaner

Daryl I didn't do it.
Jill No. You wouldn't.
Daryl How do you know?
Jill Paracetamol and whiskey.
Daryl Where?
Jill Under the bed.
Daryl Why didn't he lie on top? Much comfier ...
Jill Do you know him?
Daryl No! I've never been here before.
Jill I don't think he's been dead long. There's no smell.

Daryl starts feeling sick again and looks for the bucket

Jill You leave Jack alone.
Daryl That's why I couldn't ... You see ... Couldn't let you go and you told them and they thought I did it. But now you know he did it and I didn't, you won't tell them.
Jill We can't leave a dead body decomposing on the King's Road.
Daryl Can't we?
Jill I've got the keys and I've cleaned the windows so they'll know I've been here.
Daryl But I could go.
Jill No because they'll find your finger-prints, and you've got a criminal record, so they'll know you've been here. You've got to *say* you were here.
Daryl I was just passing, tried the door and found it wasn't locked so thought I'd go in and steal something but I found a body instead. Can I be done for that? Not stealing anything?
Jill Yes if you intend to steal something.
Daryl How do you know?
Jill With intent. That's a legal expression they do people with. There has to be a proper reason for you being here.
Daryl What? (*He thinks*)
Jill We're both window-cleaners
Daryl Are we?
Jill And we've come to do the house together. Partners.
Daryl Yes

Jill What's your name?
Daryl Why?
Jill You're my partner. I need to know your name.

Beat

Daryl Daryl.
Jill That's nice.
Daryl Is it?
Jill Your mum choose it?
Daryl Yeah.
Jill What does she think of you being a burglar?
Daryl She wanted me to be a teacher. That's a laugh. I hated school.
Jill Tell her — you're a window-cleaner.
Daryl I could go and visit her again.
Jill With Fred.

Daryl looks at Jill

There's changes. If the courts give you more time with Fred and your wife won't let you see her, they're going to make her do community service.
Daryl What's that?
Jill All sorts of things, picking up litter, shopping and cleaning for old people, weeding the parks ...
Daryl With her fingernails?
Jill Exactly. You'll have all the days you want rather than her break her fingernails!
Daryl Hah!
Jill I didn't *say* I had a partner.
Daryl No.
Jill To the agent.
Daryl No.
Jill But I'll tell them, with business expanding I was giving you a trial.
Daryl Thank you.
Jill You'll have to work hard.

Daryl I will.
Jill And we find a body.
Daryl And?
Jill We ring the police.
Daryl Yes.
Jill Like honest citizens.
Daryl Yes.

Beat

Jill Can I have my phone then?

Beat

Daryl Use theirs.

Jill picks up the receiver. Daryl holds down the connecting button

How do I know what you're going to say?
Jill I've just told you.
Daryl You're going to yell for the police and do me!

Daryl pushes her away from the phone

Jill You ring the police.
Daryl And what do I say?
Jill I've told you. You've got to. Otherwise you'll get done for burglary again and probably for contributing to that man's death — he was just up to *here* with being burgled — and you'll lose your day with Fred, and I'll tell them you assaulted me.
Daryl I didn't.
Jill You bucketed me!
Daryl You bucketed me!
Jill Do it.

Daryl reluctantly picks up the phone and dials 999

Daryl (*into the phone*) Police.

Jill starts to unpack his sports bags

Daryl (*into the phone*) We came to window clean and found a body. Dead, yes. (*To Jill*) Where are we?
Jill 23, The Pallants. Near the King's Road.
Daryl (*into the phone*) 23, The Pallants near the King's Road. Daryl Greenwood. (*He looks at number on the telephone; reading*) 328 4415. (*He replaces the receiver*) They're coming.
Jill (*indicating the loot*) Wipe that stuff. Put it back. Get your hands in the water — get 'em roughened up.
Daryl Can't we use rubber gloves?
Jill We could, I suppose.

Daryl hands Jill the rubber gloves

Daryl Your eyes are all right.
Jill Washing-up liquid's as good as anything, warm water, and cold to rinse, and you dry and shine with old newspaper ... Look at the result ... Are they?
Daryl Blue.

THE END

FURNITURE AND PROPERTY LIST

On stage: Sofa
Drawers. *In them*: valuable/stealable items, around two thousand pounds in twenty pound notes
Telephone. *On it*: home telephone number
Sports bags
Window-cleaning cloth for **Jill**
Ladder

Off stage: Bucket with the word "Jack" painted on it (**Jill**)
Rubber gloves (**Daryl**)

Personal: **Jill**: tissues, mobile phone

LIGHTING PLOT

Practical fittings required: nil
1 interior with exterior backing behind windows

To open: General interior lighting with daylight exterior behind windows

No cues

EFFECTS PLOT

Cue 1 **Daryl** exits to the bathroom. Sound of retching (Page 2)
Toilet flush

Cue 2 **Daryl** and **Jill** exit (Page 22)
Mobile phone ring

www.ingramcontent.com/pod-product-compliance
Lightning Source LLC
Chambersburg PA
CBHW070453050426
42450CB00012B/3258